Healing Your RAD Child

By Faye Snyder, PsyD

© 2012 by S. Faye Snyder, PsyD.
v1.2.120512

ISBN 978-0-9854714-5-3 (paperback)

All rights reserved. No portion of this document may be reproduced – mechanically, electronically or by any other means – without the permission of the publisher.

Cover Design: Lisa Wiscombe

Clifton Legacy Publishing
Los Angeles, California

Printed in the United States of America
First printing November 2012

TABLE OF CONTENTS

1: Identifying the Problem 5

Creating RAD 5

Recognizing RAD Symptoms 8

Misdiagnosing RAD Children 11

2: Healing Your RAD Child 19

Relating Soul to Soul 22

To the Therapeutic Parent 42

Containing, Holding and Rage Reduction 44

3: Disciplining a RAD Child 55

Best Practices 55

Controversies in Disciplining a RAD Child 59

Therapeutic Responses for RAD Kids 64

Therapeutic Parenting Guidelines for Discipline 66

Practicing: What Would You Do? 74

Gang Think vs. Anti-Enabling Theory 80

Upon Losing Your Cool 83

Failure is Not an Option and Congratulations! 85

References 87

1: IDENTIFYING THE PROBLEM

Creating RAD

Children are born to bond and to attach. That is every child's primary, gene-driven drive. Children need one continuous, primary, attuned caregiver in the first three or four years of life. When children have so much as that, they thrive in life. I call them Twice-Blessed. As a child they are adored. As an adult they are revered.

A child who does not have a primary and continuous attachment is at risk for a number of childhood disorders. One of the worst outcomes is Reactive Attachment Disorder (RAD), which leads to other serious childhood diagnoses in latency and adolescence, as well as serious adult diagnoses later in life. This disorder is tragically under-recognized within our profession because the majority of therapists actually believe that RAD results only from adoption. The ignorance stems from our academic educations and is inexcusable. I cannot tell you the number of children I have encountered with RAD who were taken to one doctor after another and incorrectly diagnosed during the precious years when they would have been so much easier to treat. Most of these children were thought by doctors or therapists to be genetically impaired, diagnosed with Attention Deficit Hyperactivity Disorder or Attention Deficit Disorder and then incorrectly prescribed medication.

Along the spectrum of RAD you can find children who were not adopted at a young age, but were placed in day care in the first year or two of life. It is essential that mental health professionals be on alert for attachment issues resulting from Postpartum Depression, custody disputes over very young children or even the most difficult of Children's Services decisions to remove an infant or a toddler from her primary parent. It is incumbent upon mental health professionals to warn parents of the risk to the child's personality when they put babies and toddlers in day care, hiring and firing nannies or taking vacations away from one's children in the first few years of the child's life.

Most of the cases of RAD (as well as ADHD) that I have seen result from parents putting their children into day care before three years old. When parents have already put their child in day care and the child has become symptomatic, it is critical that a correct diagnosis of RAD be made sooner than later. Time is of the essence. A child is born to attach and the critical period for attachment is in the early months. Every day that passes after birth that the child is not attached further impedes his long-term mental health.

These children may develop a diagnosis of Oppositional Defiant Disorder (ODD) or Conduct Disorder (CD) before they reach adulthood. ODD and CD need to be understood in terms of origins rather than genetics. Often, by the time the child becomes an adolescent, the early childhood history is forgotten and these children are perceived as having brain anomalies or chemical imbalances due to genetic predispositions, a.k.a. "The Bad Seed Theory." These theories are supported by research that shows that these children have different brain formations and chemistry than the healthy normal child. However, this research does not recognize the other research that shows that failed attachments and other early childhood traumas do affect the shaping of the brain and the chemistry of the child, including enlarged ventricles. In some cases authorities assume that bad parenting resulted from parents who refused to medicate their children rather than from the decision to abandon one's child to day care. When a parent fully recognizes the risks, most manage to find ways to modify employment and their budgets so that day care is not necessary. Unfortunately most advisors in the parents' life, including therapists, encourage them to make the choice against nature. The only culpable parent who puts their child in day care is the one who has been informed that it is dangerous for their child, who can afford to stay home and chooses to go back to work anyway.

As these children become adults, they may develop Narcissistic Personality Disorders, Borderline Personality Disorders, Schizoid or Antisocial Personality Disorders, depending upon the severity of the failed attachment and the type of discipline they also experience in later years. Adults who display criminal behavior were most likely RAD children once. The more violent the criminal behavior, the more certain it is that the adult was once a RAD child, as well as an abused child.

Recognizing RAD Symptoms

RAD symptoms are the basis for a diagnosis. There are three primary clusters of symptoms: Fear of attachment, educational difficulties and criminal solutions to problems.

Fear of Attachment

The commitment to never be vulnerable with another human being for fear of heartbreak leads to numerous behaviors that reveal this fear. As an infant she may arch her back and push away when someone attempts to hold her. She won't cuddle or let her body go limp in the arms of an adult. She feels incapable of giving and receiving affection. She may refuse to make eye contact, especially as an infant being held by a maternal figure, and instead will create a diversion. She will point to the upper corners in the ceiling, as if they are interesting, in a flagrant attempt to "change the subject" so she won't have to be intimate with someone through the eyes. Some parents think this is a sign of intelligence, that she is "so interested in things." When she is older, she may seek to establish control by superficial behaviors, including engaging in eye contact to create control. She may even engage in staring contests. She may practice a kind of phony charm and indiscriminate affection with strangers. While she has decided she doesn't need anyone, she realizes that she does need to use adults until she is old enough to leave them. Her solution is to manipulate people. At some point this failed charm may break into a rage or demand for cooperation. At other times, clingy behavior may surface as the child's desperate fear of abandonment and annihilation shows through.

She won't learn genuine social skills and she will have poor peer relationships, except perhaps with older children. She admires older children who are tough and she may develop a following of younger RAD children who, likewise, admire her.

She may develop the ability to play adults against one another and she may learn to blackmail adults with threats to call Children's Services if they don't do what she says. When this becomes the case the adults need to have the child's attachment therapist write and seal an official letter that can be opened by a social worker or police officer, stating that she has made this threat in the past and should not be easily believed.

Difficulty Learning

Even though she is driven to use people, drive them away or cause them to retaliate, she is shocked when it happens. She may become devastated over how people reject her or fight back. When someone retaliates against her, she does not understand or see that she created their negative response. There is a lack of cause-and-effect thinking. She has also shot herself in the foot in school by concealing that she needs help understanding anything. She will act arrogant when she is trying to cover up her fear of being discovered as someone weak or unable to understand. Her extreme self-consciousness is seen as a learning disability, when in fact, she has simply missed learning a basic building block and won't reveal it to anyone.

She may also be diagnosed with ADHD as if her behaviors are genetic and she needs medication to make her manageable in the classroom. She may have abnormal eating patterns from deficient bonding and abnormal speech patterns from insufficient dialogue in her younger months. She may create incessant chatter or jabbering with persistent nonsense questions, which also drives people away.

Criminal Solutions

The capacity for impulse control develops in the interaction between the child and their primary bonded adult who offers understanding and empathy for the child's distressed emotions. Since the RAD child didn't experience this crucial understanding and empathy, she has impulse control problems. When she concluded that she didn't need anyone or owe anyone good behavior, she placed herself outside the law, so-to-speak, which, when combined with impulse control issues, gives her the idea that she is inherently bad. She may cheat or act sneaky and steal for a rainy day because she feels cheated or just because she can. She may engage in "crazy lying" when it serves no purpose except getting her into more trouble. She has also not developed empathy for others because she did not receive it during her bonding and attachment stage of development or even until now. Thus she has a lack of conscience. She has become self-destructive and a danger to others. She may be cruel to animals, play with fire and develop a preoccupation over blood and gore. She may become quite an artist as she develops her ability to draw gruesome pictures revealing her hurt and rage.

Misdiagnosing RAD Children

Because some clinicians, researchers and theoreticians believe broken or failed attachments do not affect the long-term formation of the emotional health of our children, while other researchers provide evidence that it does, RAD children are at high risk for misdiagnosis, depending upon who's looking. The field of psychology itself has a split personality, shrouded by a philosophical open-mindedness that fails to ask the question, "How can both of these contradicting claims be true?" This tolerance of conflicting research spares us the responsibility to get to the bottom of the things.

I call one school of thought "pro-child" and the other school of thought "pro-parent." Each side produces research that draws separate and opposite conclusions about the causes of mental health problems, either supporting the needs of children or the presumed needs of parents. When the question is asked whether day care or abandonment trauma actually affects personality long term, some scientists need to provide evidence that there is no such trauma or pressure on parents. Often researchers are funded to produce studies proving a given hypothesis and are offered bonuses when their research does just that. Or the researchers may be asked to table their study when they cannot prove the original hypothesis.

Pro-parent researchers often have more public relations backing like press conferences that release the information to the public with a particular spin. Some of the pro-parent forces include the feminist movement, which imposes a demand on the field of psychology to be politically correct and support the rights of mothers to leave their babies and young children in day care. Another even larger force for pro-parent research is the pharmaceutical industry, which proposes that how children turn out results from genetics, not parenting. Additional forces impacting research include the day-care industry and an educational system that only funds extra help for children with genetic disabilities. Thus, ADHD has already been cleared and relegated to conventional wisdom as a genetic disability, without any sustainable evidence, but RAD is a diagnosis that won't attract such funds since it is caused by a lack of sufficient bonding. The pro-child research demonstrating the harm from weak or broken attachments is usually valid and replicable, and often formulated with greater ethics and accuracy. Pro-parent research has dramatically more funding and a trail of fraud. The good news is that when correctly diagnosed, RAD children are not medicated as much as children with ADHD, which doctors have been persuaded to believe is genetic.

There is no overseer or sage at the top of the field to contemplate and explore the mixed messages from the right and left sides of mental health. The *corpus callosum* of psychology remains split and the research results remain incompatible. Some pro-parent research says children benefit from day care because they measure positive results by independence. The most common version of RAD, however, has a strong appearance of premature independence. The children who appear the most insecure and hyper will be prescribed pharmaceuticals due to some alleged genetic predisposition. On the other hand, pro-child research says that the earlier a child is placed in day care and the longer time they spend there, the more anxious and violent they will become. I have yet to meet a child who entered day care in the first year of life who did not become RAD.

Some RAD children are diagnosed as the Inhibited Type, while others are evaluated to be the Disinhibited Type. The inhibited children seem excruciatingly shy, hypervigilant or socially ambivalent and they resist comforting by their parent(s). However withdrawn though, they do not act particularly independent. The Disinhibited Type, which is much more common, may seek to charm a parent or a teacher and initiate affection to manipulate. However, both types will avert from affection unless it is their idea and under their control.

RAD children begin to evidence signs of oppositional behavior early in life. Since they have not been afforded an opportunity to attach to a primary caregiver, they develop contempt for authority. They may lie, steal and commit acts of violence because they have not attached, as they were genetically designed to do. They are angry and have no conscience or empathy to give because they never got it. None of us could have been anything other than RAD if we walked in their shoes. RAD children who were adopted feel freer to scapegoat their adopted parents than RAD children who live in the same home with their biological parents. In other words, adopted parents are in more danger than biological parents, for the most part. The percentage of RAD children who commit violence against parents or siblings is low, but not insignificant.

Further, RAD children are more at risk for child abuse because they are so insubordinate. They are also more at risk for being prescribed anti-psychotic medications as they grow older. Anti-psychotics have long-term side affects that can be terribly debilitating, but then that's the idea. They are designed to make people manageable, even if it destroys their quality of life.

Some RAD children may seem to have always been RAD because they were never given an opportunity to attach. Other RAD children were once sweet and responsive little ones, but they radically changed into jaded and independent children after a major attachment break. It didn't have to be anyone's fault. A mother could have died. Maybe Mom was a single parent who *had* to go to work to pay for food and shelter. Babies don't know motives; they simply decide they don't need anyone anymore and nobody will ever break their heart again. A baby who has made that decision most likely suffered Post Traumatic Stress Disorder as a result of that broken attachment. These children appear like tough little cookies, but they are our most fragile and least resilient children. Unfortunately, as they grow, they will probably be the ones to do the most harm to others.

What is under-recognized is the wide variety of circumstances in which a child may become RAD and the continuum RAD implicates. For example, a child may have been RAD from a complete attachment break at two years of age and another may be RAD because they never attached to anyone in particular until they were adopted at two years of age. Yet another child may have been in day care since they were a newborn. Each child will have a slightly different version of RAD. However, if a child had an attachment break at two years old or was adopted at six months or put in day care at one year, their symptoms will be life-altering, but not quite as severe. The severity of their symptoms can also be mitigated depending on how much therapy followed with an attachment therapist. If a child was put into day care at two years old, had an attachment break at three years old or remained with the same parent who was chronically neglectful or abusive, the child will appear more functional. Some may even escape the diagnosis of RAD, but may have severe Separation Anxiety Disorder or become diagnosed with Attention Deficit Hyperactivity Disorder. The traumas to the child become less and less significant to the diagnostician. If the traumas were just a little later in age or smaller in severity they may appear a little less visible and more acceptable, and then the child's symptoms would become characterized as temperament, if not personality.

Sometimes parents will say to me, "Well, I was put into day care from birth and I turned out alright." I silently look at them and witness their aggressive manner in winning a point and the indifference they seem to have to their own child's needs. I notice how their ego seems to be on the line and that they have developed defensiveness for their parents. It is a sort of denial built upon pretending since their own attachment is weak. These parents may seem to be a know-it-alls and appear rather dominant or arrogant, but they turned out "alright." I notice with one particular mother that she was middle-aged and had never married. Or perhaps the parent is seriously overweight. "You did not turn out alright," I think to myself. "Maybe there were mitigators in your life that other RAD children don't enjoy, but you did not turn out alright." I suppose sometimes it's about the height of your bar. I want all children to be resilient and flourishing. Given so much day care of late, many insecure children are actually "average." Why settle for average?

As I have said, most professionals in the field of psychology, even specializing in attachment, believe that the only RAD kids are foster children. They believe that children with RAD symptoms who have stay-at-home mothers cannot be RAD, but they can. The Unabomber was a RAD kid. He was put into an isolation tent for allergies as an infant at about ten months old. He came back a completely changed child and grew to an adult who hated technology on the most visceral level, and hated most of those responsible for promoting it. He did not understand his own RAD. Perhaps if he had, he wouldn't have blamed technology for his pain; he would have blamed doctors who did not understand the importance of secure attachments.

We remember hearing about Eric Harris and Dylan Klebold in 1999 for their mass murder-suicide at Columbine High School. Harris was a RAD kid who was profoundly under-supervised by his parents; he was highly unattached. According to FBI-released information on the two, Klebold was profoundly depressed, also from a failed attachment, but to be depressed, one has to have experienced loss, so Klebold was the healthier of the two.

2: HEALING YOUR RAD CHILD

The only reason Healing is introduced before Discipline is that something had to come first in print. Really, either concept could be addressed first, but it's important to understand both concepts before you begin either. They go hand-in-hand; Healing a RAD child is not possible without Discipline and vice-versa. Healing is essential in order for you to get to the heart of your RAD child; concurrently you must be able to take command and establish your authority to relieve him of the burden of being "in charge." You must earn the child's trust as you go. You must be safe. You must be fair. Read this entire work before you undertake the process so you're better-armed.

I have offered a number of approaches that seem to fit different age groups. If your child is under five, you want to work especially with Holding Therapy or Containing, in addition to Supernanny's self-restraint techniques. If your child is between five and ten, your emphasis may need to be on the biography/coach approach to follow. If your child is over ten, you may need to work primarily from the therapeutic discipline approach. If your child is in her teens, you may need to consider Wilderness Therapy. Finally, if your child has left home, then your response would be in accord with the Anti-Enabling theory and practice. I recommend you learn all of it and mix and match wherever applicable.

Before you discipline a child with RAD, you need to be crystal clear that your child is not behaving badly out of arrogance. This defiance of authority results from an early childhood moment when the child realized there was no adult in her life who could protect her or who wanted to take care of her. In that moment - perhaps even as an infant - she realized she was not safe, that she was on her own and coaxing herself out of her terror, decided she didn't need anyone anyway. This child's philosophy led her to fear vulnerability and to believe that she was, therefore, entitled to do whatever necessary to survive. The injury behind this choice was so deep that it followed a moment when the child thought she would die, and it preceded the burying of a great deal of betrayal and rage. Further, she can no longer clearly recall the moment she made this choice. The child has come to believe over time that this is just the way she is, someone with a hard heart, who intends never to be vulnerable or open to the dangers of love. Since she was too young to remember, she may not believe she ever risked love in the first place, but she did. She can never be convinced that anyone is worth trusting. Not only does she trust no one, she holds contempt for everyone, especially adults.

RAD kids often act like little mobsters (Disinhibited Type) or ever-frightened children (Inhibited Type). The Inhibited child is easier to discipline, but harder to calm and reassure. The Disinhibited child can seem very arrogant and composed or insanely defiant. They use the skills they have to survive, including lying, stealing and cheating. They cope with their rage by abusing others and sometimes even setting fires. They are attracted to other RAD kids whom they can admire. They often enjoy taking a younger child under their wing and possibly corrupting them, perhaps creating something in common. In some cases, however, a RAD child could actually be protective. They have discovered the power differential. I have come up with the concept of the power clock to give kids and adults an awareness of the role power plays in their lives. When we are at 12 o'clock we are in power and not vulnerable, while being at 6 o'clock means we are out of power, humble and open to learning. RAD kids live at 12 o'clock (in power), imitating adult behavior. There is no desire whatsoever to be at 6 o'clock (out of power). RAD kids believe that vulnerability equals suicide.

It is important to always keep in mind that your child has come to believe she is evil because she has had recurring thoughts that represent her rage and she realizes she is indifferent to the suffering of others. She thinks she was born this way. She believes her issues are genetic and that she is a bad seed. This is why it is so important to tell her the history that relates to her, so she can see she was born innocent. She is originally and intrinsically innocent. There are no genes that forbid her from unlearning and relearning her original self.

If I had a RAD child of my own, I would talk to her soul to soul.

Relating Soul to Soul

The following is the essence of the message you give your RAD child. If she is RAD because of another parent or parents (adopted) or you (whether you were misinformed, ill, depressed, emotionally injured yourself, involved in a contentious custody dispute or took an unconscious vacation), you must offer complete empathy with no defending. Modify the dialogue. Tell it your way. Tell it from the heart. Tell it 100 times or 1,000 times. Keep it on the table, figuratively or literally. She will be all ears even if she acts like she's not listening. This is the dialogue she longs for to make sense of everything, but it is also the worst thing that could ever happen because it will make her want to love you for helping her. She will be as conflicted as anyone could ever be. It is the dialogue that makes her wish it were safe to open her heart again, but she is sure that if she does, she will be so badly hurt that it will kill her. Adapt the monologue below to the child's age. Let it turn into a dialogue wherein she begins to ask you questions, challenge you and dare you to keep your word. She will test you to see if you will abandon her again. She will do worse things to see if you will change your mind. If you ever saw *The Exorcist*, this is a measure of the work ahead of you to save your child's soul. In my opinion, you have no choice.

The words below are mine, but you can use as many of them as you want as your own. However, don't seek to memorize these words. Read them again and again until you internalize the consciousness, the love, the understanding and the acceptance you will need to express to your very own RAD child. Use what I have written as a template and cut and paste. Rewrite it until it is her story.

Lastly, there are words below that are big words for a young child or words that most grownups don't know. Know that your child can learn them and they are important words for her to understand. She may learn them quickly because these words represent what she already has thought and felt. Giving her words for what is happening inside of her will make her feel seen and understood and sane. These words may be big words, but they are a gift to her. She will learn them like a child learns supercalifragilisticexpialidocious. Just teach them carefully. Use them thoughtfully, repeating them at just the right time or context; the understanding will come. Start with root words, like "heart" and "hurt," holding your chest and showing empathy, perhaps by petting her head softly. Then advance with words like "love," then "attachment," then "broken attachment." Grow her vocabulary. Eventually use words like "betrayal," "fear of dying," "mistrust" and finally the word of words: *"vulnerability."*

My Furious Child

My furious child,

I love you with all my heart and I know at this moment that you doubt me. I am also imagining you think the world is unsafe. I know you are not about to love me or give your heart away to me because you believe if you do, I will break your heart again and you couldn't bear that another time. I want you to know that I don't need you to love me. I am strong enough to love you without you loving me back, but nothing in the whole world would ever make me happier than the thought that you love me.

Do you remember when your heart got broken when you were so very little? If you don't remember it, I wonder if you think that something has always been wrong with you. I suspect that you think that I think you are bad or not good enough. I want to tell you that I am an expert on you, or at least on how good you are. I know that all babies are born miracles and so were you. You were a little angel when you were born and you were perfect. Everything was in you to become a great person who could be creative and loved by everyone who ever met you. You were as holy as anyone could be. That very same little angel is inside of you now. The only thing wrong with you today is that bad things happened to you and you began to think those bad things decided who you were or defined you. You became afraid that these painful things would keep happening. You also learned to believe that the world was a scary place and people couldn't be trusted to care for you, all because the people who were the first people in your life didn't know how to behave or how to treat a baby. Most people know better. Your first people didn't. Because of these experiences and some very sick or misguided people in your life, you came to think that the whole world was dangerous.

There are words for a child who had such bad things happen to her so young. It is Reactive Attachment Disorder. Reactive means that your body has strong reactions to your experiences, especially the ones that have anything to do with cooperating with people. Attachment is a word that describes the special bond that children are supposed to have with their parent, even though you didn't get to have this special bond. Disorder means that because you didn't get to have this special bond with a special person, you began to think there was something wrong with you, so you began to feel badly and act badly. If you use the initials, it spells R.A.D. For now, until you heal, you are my very own RAD Child. I love you so much. If there was any way in the world that I could go back in time, rescue and protect you, I would. I so wish I could.

I know what happened to you, so I want to tell you a story about the beginning of your life... (Tell her whole story as well as you know it. Even if you don't know who gave her up and why, you know that bad things had to have happened for any mother to give her child up. She knows it anyway deep down inside and the truth feels real and validating. The things that happened have nothing to do with who she is or who she was born to be. If you decide to take this text in part and adapt it to your child's story, put her name in the title, add color photos if you can and turn it into her very own hard book, something that can be done through Mac, Kinko's or an online publisher. Give her a copy for herself and keep one on the coffee table. Maybe give a copy to all her significant relatives, if it helps them understand her and what you are doing for the next one or two decades.)

This is Your Story

Like all RAD kids, you came to believe that you were alone in this world without your very own grownup to take care of you. You thought there was something wrong with you and you also thought there was something wrong with the world, especially grownups. You thought for a little while that your mommy loved you and you loved her. Then she broke your heart by leaving you for too long. For all she knew, you could die. You thought you would die too. The abandonment, rejection and loneliness were so hard to bear you might have thought you would rather die than feel this pain. Maybe you thought you were dying or about to die. In order to protect your heart you told yourself that you would be all right without anyone. You decided when you were teeny tiny that you would never love or trust anyone again. You learned that you could not love a grownup because she would hurt your heart again, so you decided never to be weak or vulnerable again.

(Paragraph Example 1) Maybe you even thought your mommy didn't think you were good enough to keep and protect you. Maybe you thought she didn't care how much you needed her in order to survive. Maybe you thought you were not good enough for her. These thoughts were unbearable, yet they were never ever true. The truth is you were perfect. She was a bad mommy, probably because she had a bad mommy herself, who probably had a bad mommy.

(Paragraph Example 2) Maybe you even thought your mommy didn't think you were good enough to keep and protect you. Maybe you thought I didn't care how much you needed me in order to survive. Maybe you thought you were not good enough for me. These thoughts were unbearable, yet they were never true. The truth is you were perfect. You were so perfect that I thought you didn't need me as much as you did. I thought you would be alright without me when Daddy and I went away on our two-week vacation. It killed me to leave you, but everyone told

me you would be fine. They didn't know. I didn't know. Sweetheart, grownups are supposed to know. I should have known. I am so so so sorry. I broke your heart and your trust and now I have to work very hard to earn it back. You see, when you were a baby, the doctors and teachers and friends out there in the world didn't know how important parents are to children. It's crazy, I know. We should have known. Now I know. Now I know. Maybe you and I can tell others together some day. I will never leave you like that again. I am so so so sorry.

So you came to hold a secret that you were inferior even though you were as perfect as any child ever born. It made you feel ashamed inside most of the time. Since you came to believe that grownups were unsafe, you learned to fear closeness with anyone because they would surely break your heart again. You couldn't take that chance because it was too scary. You thought that you had to hide the real you from others, so they wouldn't see that you weren't good enough or so they couldn't see that you were afraid. You thought you had to be tough all the time to protect yourself. You thought you had to be a grownup yourself to be safe and you even thought you had to be meaner than others. Maybe it even felt good for a while to be the one who was mean.

That Other Life

That other life ruined everything for you. You never got to know how precious you were and how wonderful life is. You didn't know that you were loveable and special. You didn't know that the real you was more beautiful than anything you could ever imagine and that the pretend you or fake you was ugly by comparison. You didn't know that pride and defensiveness drive people away and being humble makes them love us more. You thought the show you put on was better than who you really were. You thought acting strong like a grownup would make you as strong as a grownup. You thought it because you were so little and so young. I mean, what could such a little kid really know? You didn't know anything except what the grownups showed and taught you with their words and their actions. The problem was that you continued to believe the same thing as you got older. You didn't stop to question what you learned from them about yourself and others. As a tiny little boy, you made the decision and it got stuck.

That other life ruined love for you. It ruined your chance to have someone safe and special in the world to know you and adore you while you knew and adored them. Your fear of abandonment or rejection took away that safe feeling. Fear took away curiosity. It took away your ability to be vulnerable. Vulnerability is the most important state for a human being because it is that state of openness from which we learn best, grow the most and feel most caring and cared for. That's where and how people build themselves as children to become great and valuable adults. They start vulnerable and great people know how to be vulnerable when it is time to be vulnerable. They are wide open to learning. They feel good about who they are so they don't have to cover up. They are not afraid to say they don't know or to ask questions. They are not afraid to apologize or say they were wrong. Even when they become adults, they are vulnerable with people they love. They are strong inside and they feel safe all the time because they know how to choose their friends and the people in their life and they have learned to feel so good about themselves it doesn't matter anymore what other people think. They choose people like themselves with whom to have relationships, people who are kind, respectful, honest, open and courageous about doing the right thing, even when it's difficult to do. You never got to know the way that healthy and happy people live and think. It's not too late though.

Healthy people feel safe in the world and become the people that get the most love and recognition. Good things come to them. They learn the most. They grow the most. They get the most help. That's why they seem so lucky. They are the ones who grow up to have the most power in the end. They never learned to be afraid of love or weakness. They actually learned that the key to power is to be weak or at 6 o'clock (out of power) long enough to learn and be loved and cared for. That is what makes them strong. So the little boy inside got it wrong. Childlike weakness leads to strong behavior as a grownup. Strength as a child leads to weak be-

havior as a grown up. So what you thought was strong is weak and what you thought was weak is strong.

It's like there are two different worlds. One is for safe people; let's call it Adventure Land. Then there's the one for unsafe people; what would you like to call it? Hell? Devil's Island? No Man's Land? It's the strangest thing, really, because of course we are all living in the same world. But what happens is that things become what we expect. So a safe person usually lives at 6 o'clock as much as possible, but goes to 12 o'clock (taking power) to do her duty, when she needs to lead. She is kind and loving to people and studies and learns things easily. She becomes knowledgeable and everyone wants to be around her, respect her and follow her. The funny thing is, she doesn't lead because she likes people to follow her. She leads because she knows she can help. A safe person thinks she is safe in the same world you are living in. You may notice kids in your classroom who think they are safe, act safe and seem to enjoy school, friends and even the teacher.

Discovering Power in an Unsafe World

It's like the people who are treated well as children learn to act safe and sweet, and the world treats them well. The children who were treated badly learn to act mean and the world treats them badly.

But you didn't see it that way when you decided that you wanted to act tough. You thought you had discovered a miracle. Your discovery seemed to pull you out of your pain and it made you feel safe. I know what happened. You realized you could flip the switch and think and act like you were in power. It would make you safe. You didn't have to be at 6 o'clock anymore like a child. You could be at 12 o'clock like a grownup. Thinking would make it so. You became a little tough guy in a child's body and you decided you could be the boss. You tried it and it felt really good. You liked it. You decided this was it for you.

It was a huge relief. What a plan! The more you assumed power and went to 12 o'clock, the better you felt. You fooled yourself into thinking that when you were at 12 o'clock, others would admire you and you would be safe. You went from feeling abandoned, rejected and terrified to feeling tough, strong and safer. You even discovered that if you bullied other people weaker than you, you felt better and even superior. Wow, what a switch that was! What a deal! It was fantastic! Think power and you feel fantastic.

In order to go there, you had to skip a lot of steps that most grownups and kids don't have to skip to get to that place of power. You had to skip years and years of education. You gave up years and years of learning to love and be loved. You had to give up years and years of learning to be close to people and get trained by them to be someone who could do valuable things to make good money to take nice care of yourself.

You just went straight to tough. Maybe you could beat people up. Maybe you could scare them. Maybe you could get what you wanted from them by taking it. You were learning to think like a criminal because you didn't know any other way to take care of yourself. Since you knew you weren't going to love or be loved, you had to become a danger to other people. Before you knew it, you had to start pretending to know things when you didn't know them. You didn't ask questions. You faked it because you didn't want to look foolish or weak. Counselors at school said you had a learning disability. That figured, right? Now there was proof that something was wrong with you. That lowered your self-worth even more. Now you believed what was wrong with you was genetic. That means that you thought you were born mad and mean. Some people said you needed to take medicine because there was something wrong with you. It was embarrassing sometimes. So you decided to get even tougher. Even though it felt good to get tougher, the tougher you got, the worse things got for you. And the older you got, the further behind you got in school and in learning how to survive successfully in the world.

A person who feels unsafe gets mean, fake and insulting to others, so people treat her like she is bad and they avoid her and even may do things to be mean to her, like judge and reject her. No one wants to play with her or follow her because of the way she treats them, but she tries to make people treat her like the boss, as if that would work to make them want to be with her or stay with her. She wants them to look up to her. She wants to force people or trick them into being loyal to her. She tries to exercise as much power as she can. Maybe she can control things and people enough to be safe. She does this because she thinks the way to make someone stay is by force. She has long ago turned away from the idea that people choose people by how those people treat them. She is not about to be nice because that would be what? Vulnerable. Yes, vulnerable. She didn't learn that the greatest power in the world comes from strategic vulnerability. She learned that the worst thing in the world ever is to be vulnerable. Now she is her own worst enemy because she fears vulnerability.

Making You Safe Again

My child, my child, I want the world to treat you well. I am so sorry that I am here to protect and teach you so late in your life. But here I am. I am going to help you get off the path you started when you decided you didn't need anyone. I am going to help you be safe and become a safe person with whom to be. It will be hard. We have a lot of work to do, but it will be so rewarding and it will be easier than the life you are facing. I will help you now. The more you let me help you, the sooner we can get over on the path that leads to success and lots of happiness.

Here's how we start. I want to make your world safe for you. I want to do this so I can help you find 6 o'clock again. I want to help you find vulnerability and the love of learning again. I want people to love you and enjoy you as much as I do. I want you to learn to enjoy people and know how to protect yourself when they hurt you. I want you to learn how to believe in yourself all the way to your core, so no one can ever define you again. I want to earn your trust by being your steady grownup. I want to model good ethics for you. I want you to see how people like me because I am nice to them. I want to be strong for you and good to you, but I will have to be the one to stop you from making wrong choices. I will do that because I love you. You will think I am trying to hurt you, just like grownups do. You will think that I am against you, like you were sure I would be. But it's not true. I will be protecting you from doing wrong and protecting you from harm, until you can make safe choices for yourself. I will also have to be a parent and give you consequences for wrong choices, but I will never do it without loving you. You will never lose me because I give you consequences for wrong choices.

I will make it safe for you to give up your big suit of armor so you can work on growing and discovering the way a child is supposed to be. Maybe when no one is looking you can check out what it feels like to feel soft inside. Look for that feeling and you will see how good it feels. It is the greatest feeling in the world. Find it. Start when you are alone.

(This may be a good time, depending upon your child's age, to take a break and read *The Knight in Rusty Armor*. It is a book for about age nine or ten and older.)

Choosing Your New Life

I know that it seems to feel better to be the one at 12 o'clock instead of 6 o'clock. I know that we imprint the way we are treated and when we go to 12 o'clock, we start treating other people the way we were treated. The question is, do you really want to treat others the way you hated being treated? Maybe the answer now is yes because it's easier to be the perpetrator than the victim, but I intend to help you find a way to get your anger out, to be safe and not to have to abuse anyone.

I understand that you often feel drives to rage and get even with someone, probably someone innocent, but I can help you learn to reduce these drives. That's a real choice. We will have to get all the ugly rage and betrayal out of your body. I will help you learn that the fear of feeling old hurt feelings makes them worse. Accepting a feeling and letting it out turns out to be quite easy, almost as easy as falling off a log, once you stop fighting the feelings. By letting yourself feel it again, you find real courage, not fake, mean courage. This is the kind of courage it takes to face old pain. It will seem scary, but it's just old feelings. Nothing bad is threatening you now, just memories. You can scream, cry, yell and tell me off for leaving you [or tell off your birthmother for leaving you or for not protecting you]. You are going to give all that anger back to me because I can take it [because I hurt you the most]. We can set it up so that you rage at this chair and you can put the mommy who hurt you here in the chair in your imagination. I will stand behind the chair and listen to you and receive your anger. Other times, I can hold you when you need to rage and receive your anger from you. I will give you back love. Dark comes out, light goes in. The more we do this, the weaker will be the drive to get revenge or to be mean.

You would need to choose to be vulnerable and let yourself feel the pain you felt when you were little, while I sit with you. You can talk to me about how you felt then and how you feel now. That means you have to feel it again, but this time you have a voice and this time it begins to leave your body when you talk. This time you will feel someone caring and loving you as you share your feelings. Choosing to relive your injuries to heal is an honorable and courageous choice. It is the better choice than hurting someone else the way you got hurt. Choosing to scapegoat someone who didn't hurt you when you were little is the weak choice. I know it may feel like no choice at all to be courageous when you want to vent. To withhold that drive to vent or to be willing to remember your pain is so worth it and it makes your life easier in the long run. It also is a way of developing your courage. It's a choice we will make together again and again, whether to bully another weaker person, to boss a grownup or to let yourself do the right thing to heal. We will be talking about that choice hundreds of times. There is only one right choice and that is health, happiness and the real path to real safety.

My job is to protect you from the world and to make you safe. My job is to understand you in a way that no one else can understand you. My job is to take care of you, even though you are sure you don't need me. I want that job and I take that job because I believe – no, I know – that you need me. You need me if you are to turn out to be the person you were born to be, before all these bad things started happening to you. I am going to be the person who helps you get back on track to being a real child, not a pretend grownup, so you can start growing again.

Since the people who win in the world are the ones who let in the most love, I want you to have that skill. I want you to know how to let yourself become weak when it's time to let down. That's another skill. It's a skill to let yourself be vulnerable when it's time to be vulnerable so you can learn again. I want you to be able to do that. I want you to find your real self and let her be. I want to make it safe for you to be you. I want you to choose the life you were born to have. When you choose it yourself, your work will go faster.

Making New Choices in Your New Life

I want you to think about what kind of life you want, how you want to act and how you want to be. Let's re-invent you. I am hoping you decide to make the choice to climb out once you believe I can be trusted. Even if you don't decide yet, I will still help you do the right thing when you don't feel like it. You may hate me for that, but I don't mind. Even if I mind for a short while and even if you can hurt my feelings I will step away and remind myself of who you really are and how much I want to help you. This same way, when someone hurts your feelings, you can step away and remind yourself who you are and who you want to be. If you see me step away to take care of myself, you will also see me come back ready to take care of you again. I hope you don't want to test me forever though. It sort of doesn't really make sense to be mean to the one person who wants to be good to you. I know you have to prove to yourself that I won't bail, but after you think I have shown you my commitment, can you begin to believe it?

If you make wrong choices, you will not lose me, but we will have to figure out a way for you to pay for it. That is what I would do and that is what we do in this family. It's also the way the world works. The world asks us to earn good things and pay for bad things we do. Then we figure out how to be weaker or sorry, so we can be smarter and stronger. That is, we will practice how to stop and search our soul so we can find the answers we need to be safer and better in the future.

I believe in honesty. I believe in kindness. I believe in doing the right thing, even when it takes more courage than I think I have. I am going to model for you good values to the best of my ability. I believe in apologizing when I am wrong. I believe in taking responsibility for everything that happens to me. That is the Strong Formula. If you take responsibility for everything that happens to you, you will get better and better and better.

So the little child in you has a dilemma. The choice she made when she was only one or two years old was out of fear, not out of knowledge. When you gave up being vulnerable to stay safe, you gave up learning and growing. Also when you made that choice then, you didn't know that we would be sitting together one day like this. You didn't know you would finally have your very own grownup who would be completely dedicated to you and love you with all her heart. You didn't know that this very own grownup of yours would never leave you unless something happened to her. And nothing is going to happen to her. I'm not going anywhere. I am here to stay and take care of you. It's what I want to do more than anything.

Learning to Handle Yourself

Now, what are we going to do about how to handle your hurt feelings when someone is mean to you? The first thing we are going to do is to make sure you understand that the nicer you are to people, the nicer they will be to you. I will be nice to you so you have a model of how to be nice. Then you will be nice to others and they will be nice to you.

But the day will come when someone is not nice to you because it happens to everyone. It will hurt you deeply where you never wanted to be hurt again. You will feel rage because you have that sore spot inside. Together we can devise a plan on how you will handle yourself when that happens. Maybe I will put you in a karate class so no one can ever bully you when you are practicing how to live without bullying anyone else. Maybe you can learn how to stop them and warn them before hurting them. I can have you tell your teacher and then me. I can have you ask to come home right now! We can have you write about how you feel. I can teach you the words you need to tell someone to stop. I can teach you how to avoid people who hurt you, even if they seem like someone you want to like you. You can learn 100 ways to tell someone to stop. But first I will try to make you safe enough to grow and learn before you have to help yourself with mean people. The point is you don't want to be around anyone who is so injured that they act mean and you don't want to be the one who acts mean. I don't want you to be the kind of person other people need to avoid.

I can help you figure out if there was something you did to invite them to say what they said or do what they did. When you can figure out how you create the way people treat you, then you will have lots of power, true power.

One of the problems from being RAD is that you have trouble with cause and effect. You only notice what other children or people do to you. You don't notice what you do to them to make them want to do what they do to you. If we are mean to someone, they may be mean back. If we are nice to someone, they may be nice back to us. When bad things happen at school, we have to figure out how it started. Actually, my child, this is the biggest hurdle with the greatest growth of all. If you can start to figure out your part, you will have done more than half of your healing.

You may want to lie to me. You may think, if I know what you did, I won't love you anymore or want to protect you. Nothing you do can stop me from wanting to protect you. I can help you more when you tell me the complete truth and together we can figure out what you did to create the problem so we can brainstorm on a better way.

To the Therapeutic Parent

The Controversies in Healing Techniques

The treatment of RAD children, who without treatment could likely become criminals or highly disturbed adults, has been an educated experiment. The learning process and dialogue continue. When normal healing and discipline techniques do not work for RAD children, experimentation has been the mother of invention.

Re-Birthing a RAD Child

There are numerous controversies surrounding treating RAD kids. One that made the newspapers was the re-birthing scandal that involved a non-therapist having a child navigate through a pretend birth canal. On that occasion the child suffocated and died, but not before trying to tell disbelieving adults that she couldn't breathe.

There are no bad guys here, only heroes. I don't even think the birth canal idea was such a bad idea, but it was implemented recklessly. I say that because I knew a child who wanted to be born to her step-mother, at least symbolically. She made it happen with a sort of ceremony of crawling under the sheets to the bottom, out and over the top into her arms. It was a turning point in her life. We are all learning from each other's mistakes and I love everyone involved in these controversies because we are pioneers sharing insight into the dangers of attachment breaks and failed attachments. It's a lonely world out there, even amongst psychologists. We are treating the children that others consider bad seeds. We are the ones actively caring about these kids making mistakes while we pioneer and discover solutions.

Containing, Holding and Rage Reduction

Holding Therapy or Rage Reduction, as others have called it, has been around for a long time, perhaps since humanity began. When I began doing it, I thought I had invented the concept and began calling it Containing. I have not adopted the other terminology since realizing others had also discovered it because I do not agree with the entire practice they each employ. One exception is Martha Welsh, who uses a clean version for normal children to unattached children, calling it Holding Time. It is a natural healing technique that I believe is not the property of psychotherapy. It is an intimate process of helping a child release built-up painful emotions, which leads to a re-bonding process.

The techniques of Holding Therapy and Rage Reduction have been used by professionals for children who have RAD and more serious trauma and behavioral problems, many of whom are on their way to becoming killers, rapists or other types of criminals. In some orientations, therapists hold the children. In the final stage at the end of holding or containing, when the child surrenders, the child bonds, or rather, re-bonds. It would be inappropriate for a child to bond with the therapist who then sends her off with her parent or foster parent, thereby abandoning her again.

Some theorists have added abuses to the treatment (elbowing, pinching, nose holding, blindfolding) for the sake of expedience so the work can be done on schedule, or to get these children to give up defiance/independence and to cling, instead, to the grownup for protection. These additional intrusive techniques are abusive, unacceptable and unnecessary.

It is a valid therapeutic goal for young but dangerous and domineering children to learn to cling to adults for protection. Older, defiant or dangerous children may benefit from wilderness camps where they have to learn to depend on a leader and their teammates for survival.

Function of Containing
- This is a way for a traumatized child to get her feelings out and heal.
- This is a way for a repressed child to break out and become authentic.
- This is a way for an under-bonded child to break through anger about trust and re-bond.
- This is a way for an unprotected child to prove to herself that her "weak" parents are strong after all.
- This is a kind way to respond to a tantrum, when the parent intuits that the tantrum is from feeling overwhelmed by an emotion or experience (such as injustice or sibling rivalry).

PaRC's Approach to Containing

I discovered Containing intuitively and did not know another term for it for many years. I borrowed from the analytic terminology and called it Containing, which refers to the therapeutic environment as a "holding environment" that "contains" the feelings of the patient, accepting all of them without defending, debating, controlling or rejecting. The therapist simply holds or contains these expressed feelings unconditionally. The parent does the same thing in Containing.

I see this process as also helpful for minor and early divergences into personality disorders in order to pull the children back. For example, a child who has been allowed to become rude and superior-acting by the age of three or four (in the belief that her parents are weak and unable to stop her) may need to be contained as a way of showing her that her parents are strong now. A child who has been left in day care may need to be contained to get all her rage out, assuming the parents do not intend to put her back into day care. I will continue to call it Containing because I want to differentiate it from the other systems that are tainted and because we use it for milder problems as well as extreme ones.

The Parenting and Relationship Counseling Foundation (PaRC) and I would actually like to establish a treatment center based on our model. Parents would come and stay with their child in a relaxing environment that includes a classroom for grown ups and children. PaRC has designated parents that have taken the parenting course four or more times as Master Parents. Master Parents would facilitate Containing as well as coach parents all day about how to respond to their children's extreme disciplinary problems, until the parents could handle the problems themselves.

Process of Containing
- Parent holds child in loose fence.
- Child will test parent, perhaps to an extreme.
- Child fights parent in a rage, but not completely with all her might because she secretly wants parent to win.
- Child fights and rages until exhaustion. (Ten minutes to three hours.)
- Child finally says the things she's been wanting to say, like:
  "I hate you for leaving me."
  "You can't take care of me."
  "My babysitter hurts me."
- After child reaches exhaustion, child goes into a state of grace.
- Parent pets the child, strokes her.
  "I love you. You're mommy's baby boy."
  "Daddy's here now."
  "Mommy's got you."
  "Mommy hears you."
  "Daddy knows."
  "Daddy's not going to hit you again."
  "Mommy's strong now."
  "Mommy's back."

Rules about Containing
- Never, ever contain in anger or use it as a punishment or discipline.
- Contain a child who is already exhibiting ma-

jor stress (flipping out, wigging out).
- Contain a child who won't let parents get close (who is suffering from abandonment). WARNING: Only repair a broken attachment if you don't intend to re-injure the child again in the same way. For example, if you left for a week and will be leaving again, do not set the child up to trust you again if you are leaving again.
- Always finish. NEVER EVER stop before you finish. If you stop prematurely, you may create more mistrust, especially if the child sees you as too weak to set limits or protect her.
- Be prepared.

Three Primary Positions for Containing
- Child sits on parent's lap facing in. (perhaps younger child)
- Child sits on parent's lap facing out. (safer for parent)
- Parent sits on the sofa, child's head in her lap, legs outstretched. (older child)

Preparation
- Get a letter from your child's therapist to keep with you or photocopy these pages. You can also send a registered letter to yourself to prove forethought.
- Tell neighbors if necessary. Some parents even inform the police that they are doing a healing process, not abusing their child. Know that Containing looks like abuse to outsiders. Ex-

plain the process to whoever is relevant. Someone intervening can be very detrimental because the child may believe her dark side won and is stronger. Or the child can discover another way to blackmail her parents. She may say, "If you boss me, I'll call the police," or, "If you contain me, I'll call the police and tell them you are abusing me."
- Make sure your mate is supportive and will not come home and demand an end to the process.
- Remind yourself that you are not abusing your child; you are healing her. Those of us who have been conditioned to avoid expressing feelings will have the most difficulty doing containing, but it will be good for us too.
- Have a coach available by phone, so keep the phone within reach.
- Understand that children who are being contained may try to fake you out or manipulate you by telling you that you are hurting them (be careful and clear that you are not), that they have to go to the bathroom when they just went; that they need a drink of water when they just had some, *etc.* Do not abuse your child by denying them their needs, but don't let them down by becoming their fool.
- Ideally, you need to let your child go to the bathroom shortly before you begin. If your child says he needs to go to the bathroom, you may let him go once or at reasonable intervals. Some children won't tell you they need to go and will save up urine so they can pee on you. It's a test; don't over react. You may want to

choose the kitchen floor or put a rubber sheet under you.
- She may say she needs water. Have some ready beside you.
- She may bite you. If your child was severely injured, you may want her to get as much anger out as possible, in which case you can wear long thick sleeves. You can make a no-biting rule or a no hair-pulling rule, although don't make too many rules. Hitting, kicking, swearing and screaming must absolutely be okay.
- Do not turn this into a philosophy that a child can tantrum to get contained. This is a special time for healing, not an interaction technique.

Containment Agreement

I, _____, hereby acknowledge that I have taken Lecture # 3, Healing, of The Miracle Child Parenting Series and that I have completed the entire series. In this lecture I was taught about the principle of cathartic healing and The Causal Theory healing method, Containment, also known as Holding Therapy or Rage Reduction or Holding Time.

I understand that Containment is to be used in order to heal an injury for which it appears that my child persistently acts out. Examples of such injuries are real or imagined abandonment, parental inattentiveness in the first years of life creating an avoidant attachment, ambivalent attachment, separation anxiety, abuse of many kinds, repression and weak or inconsistent limit setting.

I understand that Containment is a centering technique for young children, it is also a healing technique to be used by a parent who has neglected or abused their child, however inadvertently, or who by proxy, wants to help heal their child from such experiences.

I understand that the child who fights Containment also displays signs of wanting Containment. I appreciate that it only works for them if they get to fight it, as much as they wish to be contained. Because they wish to fight it, they may resist acknowledging that they want to get their feelings out. Thus I understand why my child may send me mixed messages or resist Containment.

I understand that before I use this technique, I commit to never re-injure my child by repeating any injury for which this work shall be done. Containment is not to be used to dominate or subjugate my child or to use as a means of discipline or punishment.

I agree never to use Containment in anger. Furthermore, I acknowledge that Containment is to be implemented with a loving consciousness as a reparative measure for my child(ren).

I will not retaliate, stifle my child or blame my child for raging at me or for accusing me of things about which I wish not to be reminded.

I understand that I am not to deliberately precipitate events that may lead to Containment, unless it is to express tenderness and affection to my child while holding her.

I understand that the "fence" with which I hold my child must be firm enough to prevent escape and loose enough to allow struggle and to avoid causing any pain.

I will provide myself protection by choosing a position that is safe for me, as I have been taught many positions for different ages of children.

I may wear protective clothing, gear or pillows if I think my child has the ability to hurt me.

I further acknowledge that Containment is not a method of teaching violence to children, but rather a way of relieving my child of pent-up rage once and for all. I warrant that I am emotionally strong enough to endure my child's rage against me.

I will clearly explain to my child that Containment or "going in the fence" is the only time he or she may hit, blame, rage or retaliate for early childhood injuries. This rage work will be in the context of Containment alone, when it is announced and at no other time. Any other time, the child must use her words and relationship skills, which I ensure that she or she is learning.

If any questions arise resulting from practicing Containment, I will consult with a parenting coach who is an expert on Containment or Holding Therapy, or a Causal Therapist at PaRC, (818) 891-8477.

I understand that I need to notify any adult partners, roommates or nearby people of what I am doing in case they imagine that my child's raging results from child abuse or that I am being abused by my child.

If anyone in my life is questioning the process, I will release permission to my child's therapist or my parenting coach, if I have either, to provide information about this work so there is not an unnecessary misunderstanding. I will keep handy and readily provide reading materials as well.

I have been warned that it is my responsibility to consult with any adult who shares responsibility for my child's well being about Containment before I practice it. I agree to get their written consent. I realize that in order to do this, I may have to explain what Containment is, how it works, how it doesn't teach violence to children, nor is it abusive when practiced correctly. Rather, it is a state-of-the-art, somewhat popular healing tool based upon the principles of catharsis and enlightened witnessing from Attachment and Trauma Theory (see References).

I also understand that there is a body of psychotherapists and theoreticians who do not understand how Holding Therapy can be correctly used, yet they speak against it.

Lastly, I accept complete responsibility for this work and have no intention of representing to anyone that I am a victim of my child.

(signed)_____(date) _____

Please consider signing the agreement and mailing it to me before you begin containing your child: Dr. Faye at the PaRC Foundation, Ste. 210, 15650 Devonshire Street, Granada Hills, CA 91344. It will protect us both.

3: DISCIPLINING A RAD CHILD

Best Practices

It is important to understand that you need to praise as much as you discipline. This will establish a desire in the child not to disappoint you; a child doesn't think they owe good behavior to someone who doesn't care for them. I understand that RAD kids can try our patience more than anyone can. You may not even be able to think of anything to praise, but you can. You can praise how he breathes or walks, if you are at a loss. Catch him doing something good (Thomas, 1997). Catch him doing something well. You need to develop a desire in the child to please you.

I have appreciated the techniques of Dr. Phil, but I believe if a parent wants to see effective discipline modeled, they should watch as many episodes of *Supernanny* (with Jo Frost) as possible (full-length episodes can be viewed online). I have watched her teach discipline to parents of young RAD children even though she did not diagnose them or help treat the original injuries. Nevertheless, she taught these parents how to be effective parents, if not therapeutic parents. I find her technique is compelling and I have unequivocally watched her successfully apply this technique to RAD kids. She is able to get the corrected behavior from a RAD child and that is such a head start. I have noticed when I tell parents about her technique, they often say, "Oh, sure. I watched her show. She uses a time-out technique. We've tried it and it doesn't work." I want to be clear about this: Technique is paramount. It must be applied precisely as she models it. Study it *ad nauseum*. Be ready for a test.

One of the worst symptoms in RAD children and the adults they become is a lack of impulse control. Jo Frost's technique teaches impulse control even more than it offers consequences. This is a critical skill for RAD children to develop.

Together with the child(ren), parents compose and post a list of House Rules such as "No hitting, no lying, no cheating, no stealing, no name calling, homework before play, *etc.*" The parents explain that there will be a consequence for breaking the rules and the child will first be told to stop if the child breaks the rules. If they don't stop they will be sent to the Naughty Chair (or Naughty Point or Reflection Room or whichever name sticks). Of course the child must test this. When parents witness a child break a rule, the parent warns the child if they do it again, they will be sent to the Naughty Chair. Almost without fail, they do it again, usually in plain sight.

The parent gets down low at eye level with the child and says, "I warned you and you have broken the rule. Now, you must sit on the Naughty Chair for X minutes (one minute for every year of the child's age)." The parent will then escort the child to the Naughty Chair, and in some cases will have to carry her there. I believe there is another variation in which the parent escorts the child to the Naughty Chair and then explains why she is there.

After explaining and taking the child to the chair the parent gets up, walks to the clock and sets it, turns her back on the child and walks away, GIVING THE CHILD THE OPPORTUNITY TO DECIDE TO STAY, This is their opportunity to wire in impulse control, a critical life skill. At some point, perhaps when the child comes into view or when the parent turns around to check, it becomes evident that the child has left the Naughty Chair. The parent returns the child and says only once, "I told you to sit on the Naughty Chair and now we will have to start the time over." The parent resets the timer within the child's view and then walks away again without further dialogue.

When the parent observes that the child has left the chair again, she returns the child to the chair WITHOUT DIALOGUE, NO MATTER

WHAT THE CHILD SAYS, then resets the timer and walks away again.

This is a drama that may go on for hours. It must take place without dialogue. It doesn't matter how long it takes. It is critically necessary that the parent win.

When the child finally stays the X number of minutes, the parent approaches the child, stoops to eye level and says, "Mommy put you on the Naughty Chair because you <insert reason here>. Tell Mommy you are sorry." When the child expresses remorse, the parent gives the child hugs and kisses signaling that it is over, completely over.

This must be done every time until the child learns to behave. The same technique is applied to bedtime rituals too. Every time the child gets out of bed, you walk them back without speaking.

This technique works best in conjunction with your healing work. Alone it does not teach authenticity *per se*. With this self-discipline in place, the child can still feasibly become a sociopath because sociopaths know how to behave. They just misbehave behind your back or under your nose if they can get away with it. However, this is a powerful foundation for going forward. The child has learned self-control, surrender and respect for your authority, and you have modeled patience, strength and non-violent persistence.

As you can see, healing a RAD child takes enormous discipline on your part. You need to plan to have an assistant if possible; hopefully your mate and you can start here.

I recommend you get this part in place before you begin the soul-to-soul dialogue, unless you think the child is ready to hear you already, in which case you can begin both processes of Healing and Discipline. The preceding information may be more relevant to younger children and the following material may be more relevant for older children.

Controversies in Disciplining a RAD Child

Discipline will not matter to a child if she does not wish for your approval. In order to develop a taste or addiction to your approval, you have to give enough for her to value it. As a rule of thumb we must always show and provide more love and approval of a child than discipline, otherwise our discipline will eventually drive the child away.

The latest controversy is this: One camp says give the child natural consequences for abusive and illicit behavior. The other camp says give the child empathy, understanding and guidance when she commits a crime because she only commits the crime out of anxiety or terror. Both camps teach about the terror a RAD child feels, along with her fear of vulnerability. A child cannot re-attach without becoming vulnerable. She is designed to learn in a vulnerable, open and receptive state during the learning years. Both camps notice that the child resorts to aggressive behavior in states of anxiety by acting like a little mobster. I am rather in the middle of this controversy. My equivocation is regarding the recognition of power and powerlessness, something every RAD child understands exquisitely. Yes, there is suffering behind all the bad behavior. The point is that there are always moments where a RAD kid crosses the line to abuse power. To be truthful, we all do.

We all have drives to treat others the way we were treated, good and bad, and we all experience the intoxication of power. I refer to these drives as imprinting. What goes in must come out and what didn't go in can't come out. We all have to deal with our drives to do to others as we were treated, but RAD kids experience power and powerlessness more profoundly than the rest of us do. They have drives to be in power for safety's sake and also to act out their imprinted drives, taking the coveted role of the party in power. There is a comfort in being the one in power, where we get to be one up while the other is one down. This is especially true for a RAD kid when as a baby, being out of power caused the fear of dying.

Here's how I see it: There are two types of aggressive behavior: offensive and defensive. Offensive aggression I call "12 o'clock high." Defensive aggression I call "12 o'clock fright." I am crystal clear about the power clock and its actual existence in human thought and behavior. There are many states of power (12 o'clock), from the abusive parent to the good parent or coach or teacher. There are many states of powerlessness (6 o'clock), from the frightened and helpless victim to the open student. We can see the ability to be vulnerable in every great leader and the inability to be vulnerable in every dictator or tyrant.

A RAD child may be embarrassed because she thinks her teacher has exposed her for her ignorance. She may experience a rush of humiliation and, in that state, automatically ascends to 12 o'clock fright, becoming uncooperative and defiant as a cover for her feelings of shame. If we discipline a frightened child harshly, however aggressively she acted, we will compound the pre-existing injuries.

On the other hand, offensive aggression is called the 12 o'clock high because the child assumes power to initiate, seek out and enjoy subjugation and perpetration on another, weaker party. That same child may lure a younger child into a secret space and molest the child and swear her to secrecy. Even though this is a re-enactment of what the offending child suffered from the other end of the dynamic, she has crossed the line and has perpetrated for satisfaction or pleasure and she must be scolded for her actions and probably given a consequence.

The notion that this discipline or feedback would set her back devalues ethics and forgets what creates trauma. Being held to a higher bar does not create trauma. Getting harsh feedback for doing harsh things does not set a child back, especially if the feedback is swift and brief. Further, a strong response makes it impossible for two people to be at 12 o'clock at the same time.

Look for whether or not the child initiated the act for the apparent enjoyment of dominance or infliction of pain, a desire to be on the other end of a moment she once suffered as a victim.

Imprinting becomes a drive and all of us have to face the desire to enjoy the relief and even pleasure of becoming the perpetrator rather than the victim. Sometimes it is as invisible as becoming the person who employs the housekeeper as a subservient, treating her more like an object than a person because that's how we were treated when we did housework for our parents or someone else. We all need to catch ourselves abusing power at 12 o'clock so we can see how alluring it is. Perhaps we have been rude to a telemarketer or we cut off a slow-moving car. We all must learn how to surrender power when we are wrong. With such an experience we can see what it is like to give up the stance of dominance and descend into our original injury from the other end or to recall the point of view of the other. We want our RAD child to go to that vulnerable place and cry, if necessary, so she can heal.

As parents, our job is to identify the difference between the 12 o'clock fright, which is first generation abusiveness designed to cover shame or fear, and the 12 o'clock high, imprinted from victimization. In the latter, the child becomes the perpetrator and either feels relief or actually enjoys it. The child who acts out as a perpetrator develops a self-concept that she is evil. She even looks to see if you notice and are appalled. In the first situation, the child needs help coming down from 12 o'clock. She needs empathy, safety and coaching. She needs understanding and she needs guidance in techniques to self-sooth and to modulate her own stress. I would think of ways to cajole her to safety, even offering her some chocolate cake and milk. It's as if you are talking her off a ledge.

If the child has sought out a 12 o'clock high and the role of the perpetrator, the child needs the parent to briefly shame her abusive behavior, expressing disappointment in her choice, which conflicts with the imprinted message of entitlement by her own abuser. This will put her in high conflict, but it is a conflict she has anticipated and needs to process. She received one message that it was acceptable for her to be abused and now she's receiving an opposite message by her therapeutic parent, a role model who was not there to protect her in the original injury. "Treating anyone like this is not OK and it was not OK when it happened to you."

If a child has perpetrated on another child, this is a time for a scolding for three seconds, thirty seconds or three minutes, max. Children do get their values from a need to please their parents. After that, the child will need your empathy for what happened to her as well as your understanding of the inner demon with which she struggles and you too have struggled.

The trauma your child has already experienced still resonates, but that does not mean your child is too fragile for instruction or correction. Instruction and correction are not traumatic. They do not reinjure your child. You can tell your child she needs to eat with her mouth closed. You can tell her that her homework needs to be waiting for her in the morning by the front door. You can say if she forgets her homework that she has to do twice as much the next day. You can set requirements for a RAD child and still love and nurture them through their days, especially through their reactivity.

Therapeutic Responses for RAD Kids

12 o' Clock Fright (when the child is defending his fragile identity by bluster, arrogance and toughness): Rescue the child. Help her calm down. Maybe even introduce a ritual that calms her now and for life. (For example, you could make her a cup of hot chocolate and then sit with her under a special tree in the back yard. Later, as a teen, she can make herself a cup of tea and sit quietly under a tree to calm herself. Be creative, but be sure it is something the child likes.) Offer understanding first. Then offer guidance with coping techniques. Have her repair any damage she did as a natural consequence. If she broke a window, she can work to pay for it or give up such-and-such. Try to make the work of making amends and coming to 6 o'clock more attractive than the alternative of becoming a public enemy. Maybe you will even work along side her to help write the amends letter.

12 o' Clock High (when the child chooses to be the perpetrator): Administer a 30-second scolding in her face, showing your disgust or profound disappointment in a big way. You must be bigger than her. Then it's over. Show no more disgust or disappointment at all; otherwise she will not become resilient. Then remind her softly of what happened to her and how it felt. Describe the experience so vividly that you get her to cry for herself, if possible. Maybe you can get her to rage for what happened to her so she can get her anger out at the perpetrator (the only valid object of rage work). She must make amends unless she wants to give up something meaningful to her (an alternative that is far less attractive). Maybe she loses her weekly spending money or a visit with a friend. No going forward until the child is back to 6 o'clock or a cooperative state. This is jail, which is essentially like putting her in jail, whether she is joined to your hip with no freedom or must wait in jail (preferably in a visible part of the house where there is nothing to do, as her bedroom should be a last resort) until she agrees to become soft again. You have to decide which because in creating attachment, you don't want to break it with discipline. Some children are attached enough that they will go to 6 o'clock fairly quickly to come out of jail. If they are less attached the wait may be much longer and their stay in jail may continue through mealtimes. Consider visiting the child in jail and make gentle recommendations before leaving again. The food must be very plain in jail where there is also no freedom. You may even want to give her a port-a-potty in her bedroom, especially at night. But please remember this is not abuse as it is her choice to surrender. Once she surrenders, she may come out and join the family for something fun or richly rewarding. It may be a good idea to think ahead and plan an activity you know she'll enjoy.

Therapeutic Parenting Guidelines for Discipline

The key to disciplining a RAD child is more about healing the child. This means that several issues need to be on the table.

Parents of RAD children must educate themselves. Read *When Love Is Not Enough* by Nancy Thomas, *Love and Logic* by Foster Cline, *The Connected Child* by Karyn Purvis, David Cross and Wendy Lyons Sunshine and *Beyond Consequences, Logic and Control* by Heather Forbes. Also purchase the DVDs, "Captive in the Classroom" by Nancy Thomas and the book *Holding Time* by Martha Welch.

To treat a RAD child, never see a therapist who is not specialized in treating RAD. A RAD therapist will never treat the child alone without you, the therapeutic parent, because the child must not bond with the therapist and have another broken attachment. A RAD therapist teaches the parent to be the healer and facilitates the bond with the therapeutic parent and guides her. If the therapist makes an appointment to see the child alone despite information that she is RAD, you have already learned that the therapist is not an expert in RAD. Cancel the appointment unless there is no other therapist available. If you must, educate your therapist. Perhaps take her the above books and this article.

The therapeutic parent is the one to treat the RAD child, 24/7. Plan on being with your child full time or as much as is feasible to repair her broken attachment and catch her up to speed with other children's social skills and self-esteem. No one else should be bonding with your child unless you have no bond and someone else is more willing to do the therapeutic work. In that case, you may want to consider relinquishing parental rights for your child's sake to someone who is willing to do the hard work.

Everyone else, especially teachers, must have a respectful and educated relationship with the child. Give all her teachers copies of Thomas' DVDs. Teachers must not attempt to bond with your child beyond the appropriate role of the child's teacher.

Educate your child about RAD. Tell her, "You were not born this way. You learned to be this way because you were deeply injured..." (Tell the child about the injury, offering empathy and understanding through her story. Then talk to her soul to soul about how to climb out of the hole, as we have discussed earlier.)

Teach your child what RAD kids do to cope and how they become like *Pinocchio* (giving up being a real child and that the choices are unattractive) and establish that your goal is for him to become "a real boy" (or real girl), which means he will not need to be fake, deceptive or arrogant anymore to survive. For younger children, *Pinocchio* is a good book to read or video to watch that can be used as a springboard for discussion. If possible, take him to a RAD class where he can meet other RAD children and they can talk about what it's like to be RAD.

The most important first discipline step is to reward the child for choosing 6 o'clock and offer fewer rewards or less interaction when she is at 12 o'clock. Some RAD kids don't know how to be at 6 o'clock, so it may take time to get there, like learning to wiggle your ears. Help your child develop the skill for dropping from 12 to 6. It is an internal decision. You may even want to give big rewards for developing this critical skill. Maybe you could say, "If you can drop to 6 o'clock in one hour, we will go to Disneyland (or some amusement park near you)." If you give a child a major incentive, she will learn once and for all that it is a real choice. Be sure you can practice it yourself. Talk about it with her. Talk about what is threatening her and why she is acting so proud and arrogant. Ask her if she knows the first thing she would lose when she goes to 6 o'clock. Does she think others will no longer respect her? Does she believe 12 o'clock looks good and gives her self-esteem? Does she think people will mess with her less if she looks tough? Would she lose an opportunity for revenge (on an innocent party)? Teach her to self-reflect. Is she covering up feelings of shame? Did someone hurt her feelings? Define a child at 12 o'clock as weak (not tough) and the child at 6 o'clock as strong (not weak). Every time she acts like a real child and makes an effort to be open and receptive, go over the top with recognition for how strong she is.

Expect 50 to 500 challenges to test if you are really there for her. She may do something deliberate in order to see how you will cope. Never forget that you are modeling for her how she should cope when someone provokes her at school or out in the world.

Plan to bond (adoptive parents) or re-bond (corrected parents) with your child to repair the attachment breaks. If you were the offending parent and you healed enough to be the therapeutic parent, you need to apologize deeply for the injury and know that it is your karma to heal your child without complaint. Learn about Holding Therapy (*Holding Time* by Martha Welch), but be informed before attempting this holding. Do not abuse your child by provoking her in order to initiate holding. If you need to get the holding started, stroke and kiss her cheek, tell her you love her tenderly, as a loving mother. She will fight this assault because she doesn't dare believe you for all she's worth. Yet she has a secret wish to surrender while at the same time she is terrified of the injury she will suffer if she does. (See *Containing* in Section 2 of this publication.)

Now you must earn her trust. You must prove to be a parent who is strong, loving, consistent and ethical. You need to be a parent who doesn't act afraid of your child, like her victim, or blow your stack. Stay level headed. If you find this difficult, perhaps you must heal together, since you may have once been a RAD child yourself. If you think your child would really try to kill you, it's better to get some pepper spray (that your child does not know about) than to give your child up or back to the group home. By the way, do not use the pepper spray unless you see the knife flash.

Begin teaching the child another thing about RAD kids. They do things to provoke people, sometimes on purpose and sometimes by accident or ignorance, but then when the person reacts, they truly forget what they did to create the reaction against them. Or sometimes they lie about their part so you won't abandon them. You have to convince your child that you love the truth. Let her know it is critical to have a dialogue about cause and effect. The more she learns how she creates the way people treat her, the safer she will become. Ask her if she understands the concept. Does she know why she becomes safer when she learns how people react to different types of treatment? Some parents waste years teaching this concept without earnest. You will have to teach this cause and effect concept repeatedly. It seems to be a very hard concept to learn, but it is essential. There will be no healing without it.

When your child provokes someone to create pain in them, have her apologize for provoking the child, unless she does not have the self-worth to apologize, in which case, maybe you can help write a simple letter. Do not believe the child when she tells you the other child started it unless there is a witness. Tell her when she has a track record for telling the truth you will believe what she says. If your child is in the sinister state of RAD, it is more harmful to believe her (and she thinks now she can fool you and you are dumb) than to tell her you cannot afford to believe her because of her track record/reputation/karma (something she will eventually consider).

You may need to teach her that people who don't trust are often not trusted. The way she treats people affects how people treat her. When she bullies other children, especially girls or smaller children, teach her the Vietnamese haiku: "Boys kill frogs in play, but frogs do not die in play, they die in earnest."

RAD kids don't have empathy because they didn't get it. You will be giving it (so she can get it, even though it will take longer to internalize at a later age). When your child is out of control, you give empathy by showing you understand what she is thinking and feeling to do such a thing, but the consequences will be such-and-such anyway. Put more emphasis on understanding her feelings and thoughts and less on the consequences, which should be as natural as possible. Unless someone has been injured and you have to employ the 30-second scolding with disgust, you stay cool headed with a cool voice.

Always try to give more love and understanding than consequences.

If she lies, you can tell her you see she is feeling too unsafe to tell the truth or too weak (to accept consequences), so she has to do something-or-other (consequence) to make her strong enough to tell the truth. If she steals, tell her ways to make money, but make sure she pays for what she took by working it off to get her privileges back. If she cheats, have her do three times the work, etc. For example, if she rushes through her homework, doing a sloppy job, have her re-do the homework, maybe even twice. Next time sit with her. She is not ready to do homework on her own. Where there are missing basic skills (from when she was too proud to learn), teach them until she knows them. Go back, catch up and learn basic skills. If she missed out on how to make proper written letters, go back and get it. If she missed out on "i" before "e" except after "c," go back and learn it. Get flash cards. Help her become an A student at school. That will really boost her self-esteem.

Do not punish a humble child even after she committed the crime. I would say, "I wanted to take away your computer games, but since I see you so soft and humble, I think you get it and we don't need a consequence." Talk about ways to cope better and represent herself so that she doesn't have to make such wrong choices. Discipline the child's arrogance. Take away some privileges until she is back to 6 o'clock (see Therapeutic Responses above).

RAD kids may appear to have learning disabilities because they are often too defensive to learn and later too proud to show they don't understand a concept. Make sure she learns all the material she has missed. When she is being disciplined for something mobster-like, you may want to have her work on concepts she doesn't know well, such as better printing, reading, writing, or addition, etc.

Learn the difference between a child who is acting out because forces on the outside are perceived as threatening versus sinister behaviors of a perpetrator.

If she is in 12 o'clock fright, try to calm her down. Visibly become her ally in trying to turn this around. Maybe a dish of ice cream will break the ice. Try to talk in ways that seem like you are hanging out together. Adopt casual poses, not power poses.

If she is on a 12 o'clock high, give a strong mirror and then remind her of what it was like when it happened to her. If she doesn't crack and remains at 12 o'clock, send her to jail (not her room) or make her stay with you at all times until she goes to 6 o'clock and is ready to speak about what happened in a self-reflective way. She is in jail only until she comes down to 6, not as a punishment for bad behavior. Bad behavior requires rescuing or a scolding and always amends.

Practicing: What Would You Do?

Your child has just attempted to strangle another child at school, and then told you the other kid deserved it.

Find out how it happened. Was he attacked by an insult and upset? Was this more like a 12 o'clock fright reaction? If so, talk him down. If not, give your child a 30-second scolding, then ask him softly if he remembers anything like that happening to him. If you can't get him to go soft, tell your child he needs to go to jail, where he doesn't get any privileges until he gives up his 12 o'clock stance. After he goes soft, help him write a letter of apology or apologize in person.

Then, you figure out a plan for how to protect oneself against insults. For example, once my child came home from school upset about a name he had been called. So my husband and I playfully began calling each other names. We sat together on the patio trying to think of the worst insults. At first my son was shocked. Then he was appalled. Then he caught on and chimed in. Finally, we turned on him more and more. Before we were done he was inoculated. Name calling never hurt him again. Before we were done, we were crying we were laughing so hard.

Another defense is to join the bully. Take away their power by agreeing with them. "Dumb?" "I'm not dumb, man, I'm stupid. I'm so stupid, I forget my own name."

I know a RAD child who said to another kid, "You want to bully me? Who did that to you?"

Your child has started stealing lunch from other children, telling them if they don't give up their candy bars or potato chips, she will tell the teacher they cheated on their math test. Your child looks visibly ashamed because she was caught.

Tell your child you are so sorry to hear that she threatened children even more than you are to hear that she stole their food. Ask her if she wanted a better lunch or if she liked bullying other children. Ask her to remember what it was like to be bulled. Ask her to tell you a story about it.

If she seems at 6 o'clock, tell her you are proud of her for going to 6 o'clock and that you are proud to see that she knows the difference between right and wrong. Tell your child she has a choice to apologize to the children and earn the money to buy them lunch for each occasion or she will not get the privilege that you know she loves (unless that privilege is a character-building privilege, in which case think of another loss that she loves).

Your eight-year-old child molested a four-year-old child.

Call the parents of the child and tell them what your child has done and tell them that the same thing happened to your child. Once you know you can work with these parents, take the child to their home and have him tell the parents what he has done. Have him tell the child what he did was wrong and have him apologize to the child, telling the child he knows what it was like. Have him commit to do something for the child to make amends. Maybe the other child's parents have a good idea of what would help the victim feel repaired. Have him write the child a letter of remorse and apology, including how he felt when the same thing happened to him. Then offer to pay for the molested child's therapy because you were responsible for your child's actions and should have kept him home until he was healthy enough to be with other children. If you cannot afford therapy, find a local intern or clinic that will help you. Talk with your child about his behavior, thought processes, drives and memories in his own therapy and at home. You should contain or hold him to get these feelings out.

You find your child is hiding knives under her pillow.

Put a lock on her door at night until you believe she is safe. Leave a portable potty in her room, something you can get from a camping supply store. Talk to her about her drives to hurt you and who she really wants to hurt. Get her to express her rage at the absent parent who abandoned or rejected her, perhaps at a pillow or an easy chair while you stand behind it and listen as a witness.

Your child comes at you in a physical rage.

If you can hold her, let her continue to rage until she is exhausted, all the while telling her, "I know. Mommy knows. I understand. You feel so betrayed." Don't get defensive. Receive her rage with understanding. If she is bigger than you or you can't contain her rage, then make temporary arrangements to protect yourself, like calling your husband for help. Perhaps both of you can contain her. If that doesn't work, then take your cell phone into the bathroom or your bedroom. Tell her you will come out when she calms down. Then make a plan with her how she will handle her rage next time. Maybe you can purchase and hang a boxing bag or she can tell you about her feelings and you can hand her a padded bat and be her witness. Do not act afraid of your child or give her a mirror that she is too scary. Hopefully you are not going to "send her back" either.

Your son broke a window when you told him he couldn't come out of his room until he self-reflected on beating up another child.

Now you have to decide whether the consequence triggered his abandonment injury. Perhaps you need to pull him out of the room and keep him tied to you. Or you can put a board on the window that can be removed when he comes down to 6 o'clock. Perhaps you can have him talk or write about the trigger and help him write a letter of apology offering to earn the money to replace the window.

Your child was sent home for fighting with another child.

Ask her what happened and what her part was. Find out if she was bigger and stronger or smaller. Maybe you can help her write a letter expressing remorse, if it seems appropriate. Have her talk or write about the trigger, what it feels like to be in a fight with someone else, especially someone who is bigger or especially with someone smaller. What could she have done instead? Find out if she was out to bully for fun or if she felt threatened. See if she comes down to 6 o'clock to talk to you. If she doesn't come down to 6 o'clock, sit with her for a while and then leave. Tell her you will return periodically to see if she has come back to 6 o'clock yet. That is her biggest job now. If she doesn't drop to 6 o'clock within a couple of hours, you could tell her you are all planning on going to such and such place when she drops down to 6 o'clock. Ask her to see if she can find a soft spot in her heart as you talk. As soon as she gets vulnerable, praise her and ask if she can stay there for a while. Everyone, if there are others in the family, should express joy that she came to 6 o'clock to be with them, like she is a hero for doing so.

Your daughter refuses to do her homework neatly. She rushed through it so she can go out and play.
Tell her she can go out to play when her homework is neat.

Your child assaulted another child who ridiculed him for having to go to "Resource" (where children get special attention for deficiencies in academic skills).
Get the teacher to have the offending child write a letter of apology to your child (the world is fair) and tell the child's parents that a reciprocal letter is on the way. Before giving him the letter of apology, have him write his letter apologizing for hitting the child and expressing how it felt to be ridiculed. Then discuss how your child has to accept that apology.

Discuss other options for hitting someone who is mean. Consider the possibility that the other kid had it coming, but physical violence will get him in so much trouble the other child still wins.

Gang Think *vs.* Anti-Enabling Theory

Unhealthy Path	Healthy Path
Enabling wrong choices	Rewarding good choices, withholding for wrong choices
Loyalty at any cost	Loyalty to ethics
Enjoy respect and escape rules	Earn and enjoy respect
Blame others	Take responsibility
Entitlement (for having been screwed)	Humility, teach-ability
Not vulnerable (thinking it makes her strong)	Vulnerability
Lying, cheating and stealing	Honest living, working and earning
Rebelling	Self-discipline
Scapegoating	Respecting others
Secrecy	Openness
Destructiveness	Constructiveness, problem-solving

When healing an older RAD child or deciding how to respond to a family member or friend who is on a mission to self-destruct, you need to discuss and educate about the two opposing lifestyles. Your goal is to get her from the Unhealthy Path to the Healthy Path. Unhealthy values lead to prison, death or self-destruction, any of which pave a much harder road than earning one's way. Healthy values are difficult in the beginning, but she will have support if she does her best and, in the end, she will feel proud of herself and have nice things and wonderful opportunities and experiences.

Someone who follows the Unhealthy Path will enable bad behavior in others and want to be enabled by someone who is loyal to her no matter what. She will seek opportunities to show off in order to get approval with her shocking and nihilistic behaviors. She will seek to escape responsibility, enjoy and hang with her homies where for moments in her life she is respected and valued unconditionally. This is powerfully attractive to a child who has suffered an abusive or neglectful life. It is also a powerful force for drug addicts or grown children who have never learned to earn their way. When she does something to get herself criticized she will see herself as the innocent party and the other person is to blame. She believes she is entitled to good things in life without having to earn them because she has already been neglected, abused or betrayed. She will seriously consider easy, fast income. She will not choose to become vulnerable with anyone because it is not safe, even if vulnerability will lead her to healing and intimacy. She believes she has a right to lie and cheat anyone who is in authority or who has a better life. She is quick to rebel anytime someone tries to hold her responsible for failing to earn her way. She will pick victims to scapegoat so she can feel power and unload the abuse she took from someone else. Finally, she will keep secrets as a lifestyle because she has so much to hide.

The Healthy Path will allow a person to help another who is working to have a better life, but they will not help someone who doesn't do the work. They will reward healthy choices and withhold support for unhealthy choices. They have good ethics, earn nice rewards and have healthy, happy relationships. People respect them because they have worked hard to earn expertise in their career and trustworthiness in relationships. They take responsibility for their mistakes with humility and they don't assume anyone owes them anything. They have no problem being vulnerable and enjoy healthy moments of intimacy with their mate and friends. People respect them for the path they have taken and their integrity in making honorable choices. They have the strength to stand up for victims of injustice. They do the work on their childhood injuries so they won't want to scapegoat others. They prefer an open life to one of secrecy.

When parents are investing in a child or anyone, they need to adhere to the Healthy Path and never enable the Unhealthy Path. However, there is no benefit to being impatient or judgmental about all the backslides a RAD child will make. Further, it is important not to keep holding up "old mirrors" when the RAD teen is making any effort at all. An "old mirror" is when we see someone as the person they once were and not the person they are becoming. When these kids make an unhealthy choice there is a consequence, even if it is simply the face of disappointment, and when they make a healthy choice there is a reward. It's as simple as that. When they return to the Unhealthy Path, disengage and step away. There are some exceptions, such as declining to pull the plug on a hard-won accomplishment, when the sin is understandable. An example would be to not take away the car keys because your older child lied about why she was fired from her job. She will continue to need a car to problem-solve this experience. On the other hand, if the RAD child drove her car under the influence of alcohol or drugs, then you take it away.

This is not a theory of intolerance because rejection will lose the child forever. When they return to the Healthy Path, step up and praise. You can dance this dance for years and years. There is no need to set a limit on how long you will respond positively for attempting to do better. Remember these children have some strong self-defeating messages in their brains. We can be patient; we have nothing to lose.

Upon Losing Your Cool

Lastly, you may need to prepare for the inevitability of losing your cool. What are you going to do to repair yourself? What are you going to do to repair the impression you made on your child?

I believe if I were trying to heal my own RAD child 24/7, I would have a heart to heart talk with her. I might tell her something like this: "I am very strong. I am your strong mama now. You cannot drive me away. However, you can push me and push me until I say or do something to hurt you back because I am human. I hope you never push me that hard. I hope I never get that weak. I want to be a role model for you. I want you to see that even when someone is mean to me, especially you, I don't become a bully. However, if I ever do, I want you to know that it will be your creation as much as my failure. We will share the blame together. Let's try hard never to let it get there. If I think I am going to get that angry at you, I will probably take a break. Don't think I am abandoning you. I am just cooling down. This is something you can do too if someone pushes your buttons too much. However, after we cool down, we have an agreement that we will come together and have a root beer float and talk about what we like most about each other."

When you have apologized, maybe she will say something to you as well, but maybe not. Do not look for remorse in this child for quite awhile. You have to model it and she has to prove to herself that you are the real deal.

Have fun. This is going to be the most rewarding thing you ever did and you will grow so much yourself. Read and re-read this. Don't lose your way. Play chess. Be wise.

Failure is Not an Option and Congratulations!

If you have a RAD child, you have no option but to do your best to heal her. You don't get to give her up because if you quit, you will be setting her and society up for more trauma. The worst thing a parent can do to a RAD child is hospitalize them, send them away or give them back.

Once you choose your child you have a commitment at least until she is 18 years old, although when she is old enough, say about 14 years old, you can send her to Wilderness Therapy. Save up or create equity in your house to be able to do that. You need to find a way to afford Wilderness Therapy before giving up. That will cost about $35,000, but it works. The only way it doesn't work is if you don't follow through when she returns.

Get therapy for yourself if necessary. Be as strong as you need to be. You need to grow old knowing you did the right thing, no matter how hard it was. You can do it. Know that when you have done this right thing you are a hero. You have made a huge difference in this child's life and you have prevented so many other tragedies by doing so. You rock! Feel good about yourself. A movie should be made about your sacrifice, honor, courage and character. I am so proud of you for remaining strong.

REFERENCES

Ainsworth, Mary D. Salter (1978). *Patterns of Attachment.* Hillsdale, New Jersey: Lawrence Erlbaum Associates, Inc.

Athens, Lonnie (1992). *The Creation of Dangerous Violent Criminals.* Chicago: University of Illinois Press.

Barker, Elliott (2000). The critical importance of mothering [Online]. Available: www.naturalchild.com/elliott_barker/mothering.html.

Belsky, Jay. (1986). Infant day care: a cause for concern? Zero to Three. Washington, D.C.: *Bulletin of the National Center for Clinical Infant Programs, VI*(5).

_____ (2006). Early child care and early child care development: Major findings of the NICHD Study of Early Child Card. *European Journal of Developmental Psychology*, 2006 3(1), 95-110.

Bowlby, John (1969). *Attachment, Volume I.* New York: Basic Books.

_____ (1973). *Separation, Volume II.* New York: Basic Books.

_____ (1980). *Attachment and Loss, Volume III:* LOSS, Sadness and Depression. New York: Basic Books.

_____ (1988). *A Secure Base*. London: Basic Books.

Brandtjen, Henry and Verny, Thomas. Short and Long Term Effects on Infants and Toddlers in Full Time Daycare Centers. *Journal of Prenatal and Perinatal Psychology and Health* 15(4). Summer 2001.

Breggin, Peter (2001). *The Anti-Depressant Fact Book: What Your Doctor Won't Tell You About Prozac, Zoloft, Paxil, Celexa and Luvox.* Cambridge, MA: Perseus Publishing.

_____ (2008). *Medication Madness: The Role of Psychiatric Drugs in Cases of Violence, Suicide and Crime*. New York: St. Martin's Griffin.

Breggin, Peter R. & Cohen, David (1999). *Your Drug May Be Your Problem: How and Why to Stop Taking Psychiatric Medicatio*ns. Cambridge, MA: Perseus Publishing.

Burlingham, D. and Freud, A. (1944). *Infants without families*. London: Allen & Unwin.

Calfaro, John V. and Conn-Calfaro, Allison (1998). *Sibling Abuse Trauma: Assessment and Intervention Strategies for Children, Families and Adults.* The Haworth Maltreatment and Trauma Press: Binghamton, NY.

Cline, Foster W. and Helding, Cathy (1999). *Can This Child Be Saved? Solutions for Adoptive and Foster Families.* Franksville, Wisconsin: World Enterprises.

Dreskin, William and Wendy (1983). *Day Care Decision: What's Best For You and Your Child.* New York: M. Evans and Co.

Dunstan, Priscilla (2006). *Dunstan Baby Language: Learn the Universal Language of New Babies.* Audio series.

Dutton, Donald G. (1995). *The Batterer: A Psychological Profile.* New York: Basic Books.

_____ (1998). *The Abusive Personality: Violence and Control in Intimate Relationships.* New York: The Guilford Press.

Fisher, Robert (1987). *The Knight in Rusty Armor.* Los Angeles: Wilshire Book Company.

Fonagy, Peter, et al. (2002). *Affect Regulation, Mentalization and the Development of the Self.* New York: Other Press.

_____ (2001). *Attachment Theory and Psychoanalysis.* New York: Other Press.

Forbes, Heather T. & Post, Bryan (2006). *Beyond Consequences, Logic and Control.* Orlando, FL: Beyond Consequences, LLC.

Gopnik, A. (2009). *The Philosophical Baby: What Children's Minds Tell Us about Truth, Love and the Meaning of Life.* New York: Farrar, Strau and Giroux.

Harlow, Harry F. and Zimmermann, Ronald R. (1959). "Affectional responses in the infant monkey". *Science*, 130, 421.

Heinicke, C. and Westheimer, I. (1965). *Brief Separations.* New York: International Universities Press.

James, Beverly (1994). *Handbook for Treatment of Attachment-Trauma Problems in Children.* New York: The Free Press.

Karen, Robert (1998). *Becoming Attached: First Relationships and How They Shape Our Capacity to Love.* New

York: Oxford University Press.

Karr-Morse, Robin and Wiley, Meredith S. (1997). *Ghosts from the Nursery: Tracing the Roots of Violence.* New York: Atlantic Monthly Press.

Ledoux, Joseph E. (1998). *The Emotional Brain: The Mysterious Underpinnings of Emotional Life*. New York: Touchstone.

LeDoux, J. E.; Romanski, L., & Xagoraris, A. (1991). "Indelibility of subcortical emotional memories." *Journal of Cognitive Neuroscience, 1,* 238-243.

Lehrer, J. (2009, April 26). Inside the baby mind. *The Boston Globe.com*. Retrieved: http://www.boston.com/bostonglobe/ideas/articles/2009/04/26/inside_the_baby_mind/?page=full (2011 September 21).

Levine, Peter M. (1997) *Waking the Tiger: Healing Trauma, the Innate Capacity to Transform Overwhelming Experiences*. Berkeley, CA: North Atlantic Books.

Levy, Terry M. and Orlans, Michael (1998). Attachment, Trauma and Healing: Understanding and Treating Attachment Disorder in Children and Families. Washington, DC: CWLA Press.

Levy, Terry M. (2000). *Handbook of Attachment Interventions.* New York: Academic Press.

Lewis, Dorothy Otnow (1998). *Guilty by Reason of Insanity.* New York: Ballantine Publishing Group.

Magid, Ken and McKelvey, Carole (1987). *High Risk: Children without a Conscience.* New York: Bantam Books.

Main, Mary (1995). *Attachment Theory: Social, Developmental and Clinical Perspectives.* Hillsdale, NJ: Analytic Press.

Main, M. and Solomon, J. (1990). "Procedures for Identifying Infants as Disorganized/Disoriented During the Ainsworth Strange Situation." Greenberg, D. Cicchetti and E. M. Cummings (Eds.), *Attachment during the Preschool Years: Theory, Research and Intervention.* Chicago, IL: University of Chicago Press.

Main, Mary and Weston, Donna R. (1981). *The Place of Attachment in Human Behavior,* eds. Collin Murray

Parkes and Joan Stevenson-Hinde. New York.

Parkes, Colin Murray, *et al.* (1991). "Attachments and Other Affectional Bonds Across the Life Cycle" by Ainsworth, Mary D. S. *Attachment Across the Life Cycle*. New York: Tavistock/Routledge.

_____ (2000). Bonding and Attachment in Maltreated Children: Consequences of Emotional Neglect in Childhood.
http://teacher.scholastic.com/professional/bruceperry/bonding.htm.

Perry, Bruce D. and Marcellus, John (2000). The Impact of Abuse and Neglect on the Developing Brain.
http://teacher.scholastic.com/ professional/bruceperry/abuse_neglect.htm.

Pincus, Jonathan H. (2001). *Base Instincts: What Makes Killers Kill?* New York: W.W. Norton & Co.

Prescott, James (2000). "Birth and the Origins of Violence: Perspectives on Violence."
http://www.birthpsychology.com/violence/prescott.html

Robertson, Brian C. (2003). *Day Care Deception: What the Child Care Establishment Isn't Telling Us.* San Francisco: Encounter Books.

Rothschild, Babette (2000). *The Body Remembers: The Psychophysiology of Trauma and Trauma Treatment*. New York: W.W. Norton & Co.

Schwartz, P. (1983). "Length of day-care attendance and attachment behavior in eighteen-month-old infants". *Child Development, 54.*

Siegel, D.J. (1999) *The Developing Mind: Toward a Neurobiology of Interpersonal Experience.* New York, London: Guilford Press.

_____ (2001). "Toward an Interpersonal Neurobiology of the Developing Mind: Attachment Relationships, 'Mindsight,' and Neural Integration". *Infant Mental Health Journal. 22*(1-2), 67-94.

_____ (2002). "Attachment and Self-Understanding: Parenting with the Brain in Mind." Conference on "New Developments in Attachment Theory: Applications to Clinical Practice." 2003 UCLA Extension and Lifespan Learning Institute.

Society For Neuroscience (Nov. 7, 2007). "Mirror, Mirror In The Brain: Mirror Neurons, Self-understanding and Autism Research".

Solomon, Marion. (March 8-9, 2003). "*Treating the Effects of Attachment Trauma*". Excerpted for: New developments in attachment theory: Applications to Clinical Practice, UCLA.

Solomon, Marion F. and Siegel, Daniel J. (2003). *Healing Trauma: Attachment, Mind, Body and Brain.* New York: W.W. Norton & Co.

Sonkin, Daniel Jay (2005). Attachment Theory and Psychotherapy. *The Therapist Magazine.* January/February, Vol. 17, 1, 68-77.

Spitz, Rene A. (1949). "The Role of Ecological Factors in Emotional Development in Infancy". *Child Development, 20*(3): 145-155.

Stern, Daniel. (2000). *The Interpersonal World of the Infant.* London: Basic Books. (Original work published 1985)

_____ (2003). Attachment and Intersubjectivity. Conference on New Developments in Attachment Theory: Applications to Clinical Practice. UCLA Extension and Lifespan Learning Institute.

Stosny, Steven (1995). *Treating Attachment Abuse: A Compassionate Approach.* New York: Springer Publishing Company.

Szalavitz, Maria and Perry, Bruce (2010). *Born for Love: Why Empathy Is Essential and Endangered.* New York: Harper Collins.

Teicher, Martin (2002, March). "Scars That Won't Heal: The Neurobiology of Child Abuse: Maltreatment at an early age can have enduring negative effects on a child's brain development and function". *Scientific American.*

Thomas, Nancy (1998). *Rebuilding the Broken Bond, Part I for Reactive Attachment Disorder* [video]. Glenwood Springs, CO: Nancy Thomas. *Timmons v. Indiana,* 584 N.E. 2nd 1108 (Ind. 1992).

_____ (1997). *When Love is Not Enough: A guide to Parenting Children with RAD-Reactive Attachment Disorder.* Glenwood Springs, CO.: Families by Design.

van der Kolk, Bessel, *et al.* (1994a)."The Body Keeps the Score: Memory and the Evolving Psychobiology of Post Traumatic Stress." *Trauma Information Pages*: http:\\www.trauma-pages.com.

van der Kolk, Bessel; McFarlane, Alexander; Weisaeth, Lars (eds.) (1996). *Traumatic Stress: the Effects of Overwhelming Experience for Mind, Body & Society.* New York: Guilford Press.

_____ (1995). "The Body, Memory and the Psychobiology of Trauma". In Judith L. Alpert (Ed.), *Sexual Abuse Recalled: Treating Trauma in the Era of the Recovered Memory Debate*. Northvale, NJ: Jason Aronson Inc., 29-60.

_____ (1989). "The Compulsion to Repeat the Trauma: Reenactment, Revictimization and Massochism". *Psychiatric Clinics of North America, 12*(2), 389-411.

Vaughn, B. E., Gove, F. L., & Egeland B. (1980). "The Relationship between Out-of-Home Care and the Quality of Infant-Mother Attachment in an Economically Disadvantaged Population". *Child Development, 51.*

Wallin, D. (2002 August). Attachment and intersubjectivity in healing relationships. Cassedy Seminars. Skirball Center.

Watson, John (1928). *Psychological Care of the Infant and Child.* New York: W.W. Norton & Co.

Welch, Martha G. (1988). *Holding Time: How to Eliminate Conflict, Temper Tantrums and Sibling Rivalry and Raise Happy, Loving, Successful Children.* New York: Simon and Schuster.

Whitaker, Robert (2002*). Mad in America: Bad Science, Bad Medicine and the Enduring Mistreatment of the Mentally Ill.* New York: Basic Books.

Wylie, Mary Sykes (2004). "The Limits of Talk Therapy: Bessel van der Kolk Wants to Transform the Treatment of Trauma". *Psychotherapy Networker, Jan/Feb*, 30-38.

Zeanah, C.H., Mammen, O.K. and Liebermen, A.F. (1993). "Disorders of Attachment". In C.H. Zeanah (Ed.), *Handbook of Infant Mental Health*. New York: Guilford Press.